SHARON J STEIN

HOW TO FIND YOUR HOBBY

A book on finding and
following your true calling.

INTRODUCTION 3

HOW TO FIND YOUR HOBBY 10

WHY HAVING A HOBBY IS IMPORTANT...24

FIND A HOBBY WHEN NOTHING
INTERESTS YOU 29

WHEN THERE ARE TOO MANY TO
CHOOSE FROM 66

CONCLUSION 94

REFERENCES 96

INTRODUCTION

One of life's greatest privileges is the discovery of a satisfying hobby. It's an excellent method of passing the time and expanding one's knowledge base. I think it's great that people now have so many options. In fact, you can find whole websites that cater to certain interests and pastimes.

The best way to cultivate a new hobby is to dive headfirst into it. So much of the world's wonders and curiosities lie in wait for exploration and acceptance. Everyone has their own unique set of interests and activities because no two people are exactly alike. Yes, once we find something we're passionate about, we can't help but devote all of our time and energy to it. It piques our interest and holds our attention on a personal level, making us want more of it over time.

There are many compelling reasons why everyone should take up a hobby, but here are a few of the most compelling:

1. **More Interesting.** It will make you more intriguing to those around you. Hobbyists are more likely to have accumulated a wealth of information and anecdotes worth sharing because of their involvement in their chosen field. Anyone who shares their interest in their specialized fields is welcome to learn from them.

2. **Reduce Stress.** You'll be less likely to obsess over the difficulties in your life if you're using your brain on something that brings you joy. It's possible that one's hobbies can provide a welcome reprieve from the stresses of daily life.

3. **Patience.** The first step in developing a new hobby is learning about it from scratch. You should be patient with yourself as you work to overcome the learning curve and boost your performance.

4. **Friendship.** Sharing a passion is an excellent way to make new friends and deepen existing ones. It's great to have a hobby that you can talk about with others on a regular basis. Joining a league, starting a club, or simply showing off your accomplishments to others is a great way to meet people who share your interests.

5. **Confidence.** Self-assurance and esteem are the natural outcomes. When you put in a lot of effort and become skilled at something, it's because you enjoy doing it. Participating in any activity at which one excels is a great way to build self-esteem and feel accomplished.

6. **Reduce Boredom.** One of the best ways to avoid getting bored is to develop a hobby. If you're bored and need something to do, they're a great option. And they give you something to look forward to with excitement.

7. **Knowledgeability.** A person's knowledge and abilities can be enriched through their capabilities. You can gain knowledge through exercise if you're willing to put in the time and effort. Spending more time on your hobby will help you improve at it. Your efforts to better your hobby will not only help you learn new skills but will also help you learn more about the world. Among the many ways in which hobbies promote personal development is by providing opportunities to encounter and consider the perspectives of others with whom one may not otherwise come into contact.

8. **Escape Comfort Zone.** It will put you to the test. When you start doing something you've never done before, you may find yourself in situations you'd rather avoid. One cannot enjoy a hobby unless one finds it both interesting and challenging. For this reason, you should start engaging in a more useful hobby.

9. **Less Time Wasted.** Because of this, you'll have less of an urge to waste time or do unnecessary things. A common saying states that "idle hands are the devil's workshop." If you have positive things to do in your free time, you will be less likely to waste it or use it destructively.

In case you're curious about my interests, here are the top five things I'm focusing on at the moment. They're the reason why I'm happier and have a greater sense of purpose.

Reading

Books, especially nonfiction ones, are some of my favorite things ever. I've set a goal for myself to read 60 books per year, across many genres. One such book is titled *The Unconquered: In Search of the Amazon's Last Uncontacted Tribes* and it tells the story of a group of aboriginal Indians who have chosen to live in isolation in the Amazonian jungle. This fascinating look into their lives and culture spans about 800 pages in length. It's a great read that emphasizes the importance of protecting our natural resources.

Every book I've ever read (and I'm very selective) has taught me something new about the world and expanded my perspective in some way. Reading books is a great way to travel to different eras and countries without leaving my couch. The best part is that I joined the library and now have access to free eBooks.

Preparing Food

I find great comfort in the kitchen as a creative outlet. I prepare a meal roughly five times a week, and I always make a little extra so that I always have something to throw in the freezer. I've learned so much about myself and the value of patience and focus in the kitchen. Whenever I get in the kitchen, I learn new tricks and techniques that help me become a better cook. Though there have been times when my cooking didn't go as planned, I've always been able to take the lessons I learned and improve as a chef. For my own consumption, I cook delicious and healthful meals. Furthermore, it is much cheaper than eating out and, in many cases, tastes better.

Observing Natural History Museum Exhibits

I don't spend a lot of time in front of the TV. However, this rule is not always applicable, and this is especially true of good documentaries. Thanks to services like Netflix and Hulu, as well as on-demand TV and excellent networks like Smithsonian and National Geographic, I have a wealth of fascinating documentaries at my disposal. Every year, I watch 45 movies, including such diverse fare as *Craigslist Joe*, *Happy*, *Exit Through the Gift Shop*, *Somme*, and *Man on Wire*.

Physical Activity

Many years ago, I made the decision to exercise regularly, and ever since then, it's been a great joy of mine, even if some people might argue that it's more of a necessity than a hobby, like brushing your teeth. On the other hand, I find great enjoyment in a wide range of sports and workouts, from weightlifting and jogging to walking and hiking to playing racquetball and soccer. The more time

I put into it, the more benefits I reap. In addition, I've met a lot of wonderful people through our common passion.

Gardening

The use of these gardens to grow one's own food has become increasingly common in recent years. I've always had a deep love for cooking, so a few years ago I decided to indulge in my hobby by growing my own edible garden. My homegrown herbs and vegetables not only enhance the flavor of the foods I love but also provide me with healthy, organic nutrition. It makes me happy to know exactly what my food went through before it reached my plate. In addition, I have learned a great deal about the best times of year to cultivate various plants, as well as how much water and sunlight they require. The food and inspiration I get from my garden are invaluable to my intellectual nourishment.

How to find your hobby

Even though having a hobby has been shown to have positive effects on health in recent studies, many people still find it difficult to choose one. The results of these studies suggest that hobbyists enjoy better health than the general population. Here are some ideas to help you zero in on a passion project.

Childhood Activities

When you were younger, you probably enjoyed doing a lot of something. In a similar vein, you might enjoy it even more now that you're an adult. If you're thinking about giving up on something that used to bring you pleasure, don't. After that, consider your loved ones' interests and give some of those a shot. You could talk to a close relative who already follows the lifestyle you're considering adopting. Ask about their experience in the field, their availability, and the costs involved.

Try out some of your new passions and hobbies. Attempting something and failing once or twice is not the end of the world.

Interests → Hobbies

Think carefully about what you like and don't like. These include things like reading, listening to podcasts, and watching birds. Make a habit out of doing whatever makes you feel good.

You may also find new avenues of professional opportunity thanks to this philosophy. Do you enjoy playing soccer? If soccer becomes a hobby, a professional career is within reach. Evaluate your current skillset; your newfound passion could lead you in many directions professionally. If you do what you love and are passionate about, you'll never have to "work" a day in your life.

Leave Your Safe Zone

Do you ever experiment with new things? Individuals who are receptive to trying new pastimes are more likely to broaden their horizons, expand their network, and enrich their experiences. By doing so, you can test your limits, generate original approaches to problems, sharpen your perceptions, and strengthen your connections to those around you.

With such confidence in oneself, the sky is the limit. Think about the times you pushed yourself and how you felt afterward. Nothing can stop you from reaching your goals if you make it a habit to always say "yes," push through your fears, and take the next logical step.

Check Your Spending Plan

Think about the cost involved in a hobby before you start it. Some people invest a significant amount of their disposable income into their hobbies. Traveling the world, restoring vintage automobiles, and racing boats are all examples. A costly pursuit warrants reevaluation. Don't forget to factor in the cost of joining a yacht club or a ski resort, as well as the cost of supplies and gas. An excellent illustration of this is the question of how much it costs to become certified to go scuba diving. Should you buy your own scuba equipment or just rent it when you need it? Where is the best place to go scuba diving, and how much will transportation cost? Every enjoyable activity will cost you money, but some will cost more than others. When the time comes to part ways, you'll have an easier time saying goodbye if you do the math before falling in love.

Hobbies You Can Start Right Now

It's crucial to find something you enjoy doing, as this could give your life greater significance. Don't worry if you don't know where to start; we've compiled a list of some of the most common activities (as well as some less common but no less enjoyable ones) to help you get going. Read on to see if any of the available options catch your eye.

Mental Activities

Mind-challenging activities like crossword puzzles and Sudoku can be used to train the brain. Like board games and card games, low-tech brain games like jigsaw puzzles can be enjoyed on a budget in the comfort of your own home. You can take your favorite pastime with you wherever you go by downloading brain games like Sudoku to your mobile device.

Brain games and other mentally demanding activities may protect against some forms of age-related cognitive decline.

Gardening

A garden may provide a wonderful setting in which to take in some rays, do some light jogging, and enjoy the outdoors. Whether you have a tiny balcony to fill with potted plants or a vast backyard to fill with flowers and vegetables, gardening is a relaxing and rewarding hobby. It doesn't matter if you don't have a lot of money or a lot of outdoor space; you can still do it. The satisfaction of using your own freshly picked flowers or produced vegetables is unparalleled.

Planting, watering, weeding, pruning, and harvesting a garden may take a lot of time and energy, but most gardeners still find the process to be manageable and even enjoyable.

If you have mobility issues that prevent you from gardening on the ground, you may want to invest in raised garden beds or a set of pots that are simple to reach.

Feel free to expand your gardening horizons beyond your own yard. Participate in an organization whose mission is to better the neighborhood, such as a garden club.

Cooking or Baking

Why not make satisfying your hunger a hobby? While you could spend a lifetime honing your cooking and baking skills, getting started couldn't be easier. You can look at the bright side: even your "mistakes" while you're learning the ropes of your new activity will still provide you with sustenance... most of the time.

In that case, what aspects of cooking make it an absolute requirement rather than a pleasant diversion? Find out if you enjoy cooking or baking by considering whether you would continue to do it if you didn't have to.

It's best to follow recipes precisely when you're first learning to cook, especially when it comes to baking. As your self-assurance grows, don't be afraid to try something new.

Tabletop games

These activities are perfect for bringing the family together. With so many exciting new options at your fingertips, traditional board games and card games may seem antiquated. On the other hand, they are more interesting and better for direct communication between people. You can play poker, Monopoly, and other board games with your friends and family members, or you can play them with your children at a game night you host. [4]

Photography

It's easy to get started with photography as a hobby, and the results are always satisfying. Your phone's camera can take decent photos whenever you need one, so keep it on your person at all times. In the future, if you so choose, you can upgrade to better cameras and other gear. Regardless, if you're looking for a new hobby that will get you out and about, exploring the world and meeting new people, consider picking up photography as a side interest.

Beginning immediately, you may begin photographing anything that interests you. Photography is a skill that can be honed through the study of how-to books, online video tutorials, or even a class at a local community college.

Crafts

Participating in this activity will allow you to use your imagination while also improving your living conditions and lowering your monthly expenses. Despite your skill level, you can find a do-it-yourself project that suits you. It could be as simple as fixing a squeaky door, or as involved as creating your dream kitchen from scratch. Nothing beats getting your hands dirty, either in a classroom setting or by working side by side with an experienced professional, no matter how many DIY shows or websites you watch.

It's possible to save a lot of money by handling minor home repairs on your own rather than calling a professional. You can save money by avoiding the expense of a plumber by fixing minor plumbing problems on your own, such as a dripping faucet or a leaking toilet.

Don't be afraid to take risks, but also understand your own limitations. If you don't know what you're doing, for instance, stay away from the building's electrical system or framework. A savvy DIYer knows when it's time to bring in professionals.

Collecting

It's possible to collect stamps, cash, or anything else you can think of. The best part about collecting is that you can modify it to fit your specific goals and preferences. Some people stockpile items they anticipate increasing in value over time, such as baseball cards, toys, or older issues of widely read periodicals. First of all, there's nothing improper about building a collection out of pure curiosity.

Collectors often feel the need to display their treasures, which can cause problems with available space. The number of cat memorabilia you can display at once is probably limited. Set aside a specific area to showcase your hobby items; if you find that you're running out of space, you may need to sell, donate, or at the very least temporarily shelve some of your items.

Music

You can enjoy music in two ways: as a listener and as a creator. Building up an extensive record collection is a popular hobby for music fans. On the other hand, you could learn to play an instrument and enjoy music as a hobby. Try your hand at music-making or just put on a concert of your favorite tunes. Indulge your musical fervor in the privacy of your own home, the conviviality of a jam session with friends, or the spotlight of an audience.

Learning to play the guitar, piano, saxophone, or any other instrument is a rewarding hobby. It's a fun and productive way to use your mind, hands, and imagination.

Reading

If you're looking for a way to relax and expand your knowledge, reading could be perfect for you. A new hobby of reading? Certainly, why not? A biography, motivational book, whodunit, or romance novel could be just the thing to help you unwind after a long day. Reading provides you with the opportunity to do these things without having to leave your house; furthermore, it may aid in your education and introspection. One of the most inexpensive activities, especially if you already have a library card.

Writing

A common pastime, writing can take many shapes, from journals to novels. Poets, bloggers, novelists, and people who keep diaries would all agree that writing is one of the most stimulating and rewarding creative pursuits there are. No matter how simple or complex it is to put ideas on paper, writing is an excellent mental exercise.

It's fine to dive in headfirst, but if you'd like to hone your skills, consider taking a writing class at your local YMCA or junior college.

Anywhere between writing for yourself and writing for millions of people is open to you. Any option that brings you the most joy is the correct one.

Calligraphy is one of many artistic writing practices that can be practiced as a hobby.

Exercise

As a leisure activity, you can choose anything that gets you moving. Like going to the dentist, exercise can be viewed as a chore that people only do because they know it's good for them. The likes of jogging, horseback riding, and yoga can be adapted to make for a satisfying and beneficial hobby. You know you've found a new hobby if you start thinking about your next spin class before the current one is over.

Though time spent exercising solo can indeed be rewarding, many types of physical activity also lend themselves well to being shared among a larger group of people. A good alternative to riding your bike alone is to join a cycling club

Crafting

Try your hand at making something beautiful and/or useful. It's tough to find anything that compares to the satisfaction of completing a laborious craft like basket weaving or jewelry making. But how do you decide which pastimes are right for you? Discover your ideal creative outlet by exploring many different possibilities. [12]

Birdhouses, picture frames, memory collages, and even simple but endearing windchimes can all be fun to construct and embellish.

Places like community centers, libraries, social clubs, and even churches often host crafting groups and classes.

Browse the web for do-it-yourself initiatives to undertake. That's a broad question with a wide range of potential responses.

Stitching or Knitting

Depending on the individual, needlework can be a fun, challenging, and rewarding pastime. Though needlework like sewing and knitting may seem archaic to some, they continue to be widely practiced today. They're easy to pick up and play without spending a fortune, but mastery is elusive. The skills you acquire can be used to create useful and fashionable items like blankets, scarves, and garments.

Needlework in general is a great hobby, but crocheting and quilting are particularly rewarding.

Whether you're by yourself or with a group, you'll have a great time with needlework. I recommend you join or start a knitting group in your area.

If you need help getting started, look into needlepoint classes in your area.

Artwork

Engage in creative activities like drawing, painting, or sculpting. Making art has multiple advantages, including the release of stress and the strengthening of muscles. Avoid putting too much pressure on yourself to come up with a truly original piece of art. Have fun and let your thoughts wander. [14]

In general, the arts are accessible to people of varying socioeconomic backgrounds and ages. Watercolor painting is a fantastic low-cost hobby option because all you need to get started is a watercolor set, a brush, and some paper.

Your local community college might offer courses in painting, sculpture, ceramics, and other visual art forms.

Learning a New Language

Besides its practical value, this hobby could also be fun and enlightening. Having the ability to communicate in more than one language is advantageous. If you don't think you "need" to learn a new language, you're missing out on a lot of perks. What's more, it's likely to pique your interest in traveling, another enjoyable activity. [15]

You could take the typical route and sign up for language classes at a local institution of higher learning, like a community college. The good news is that there are now a plethora of online resources and apps designed specifically for language learning. Before spending a lot of money on software, think about whether you could get by with a free or cheap option.

Travel

Local or international, a vacation for fun can be rewarding. Traveling to different parts of the world and learning about other cultures is a great way to learn about yourself and the world. Seeing more of your own country is an option if traveling abroad is out of the question due to cost or other constraints. [16]

The best way to discover a new location is subjective. If you find pleasure in a cruise itinerary that includes stops at several different ports of call, then, by all means, book one. Alternatively, you could simply immerse yourself in the native cultures of the countries you visit.

Pets

Do something enjoyable with your dog or other pet. Why not combine your desire to bond with your pet and your search for something new to try? Your dog's physical and mental prowess can be judged in a variety of competitions known as "performance dog sports," in which the two of you can take part together.

One alternative pastime is visiting pet shows with your dog, cat, bird, or other animal companions. The idea is to do something fun that both you and your pet will enjoy.

Beneficial Reasons

Gain satisfaction from helping others by taking part in a worthy cause. It's possible that giving your time to a worthy cause, like cancer research or promoting literacy amongst young people, is a satisfying hobby. Contribute your time and passion to a local cause that means something to you and could have an effect on your community for the better.

If you or a loved one has benefited from an organ transplant, whether it was a kidney or another type of tissue, or if you are on the transplant waiting list, you may want to consider becoming a volunteer advocating for organ donation.

Nature

Consider taking up a pastime that requires you to spend time in the great outdoors, like rock climbing or bird watching. Spending time in nature is good for your mental, physical, and emotional health. Spending time outdoors is a great way to relax or get some exercise. It could be a stroll through the park or a hike through the woods, a day on the water fishing or paddling a canoe, or a night under the stars in a tent.

Activities centered around being outside in nature are wonderful for both introspective solo time and joyful family outings.

Tech

Robotics and programming are fascinating and challenging fields of study. Constructing your own personal robot is no longer a far-fetched science-fictional possibility. Hobbyists of different ages, skill levels, and financial means may easily locate robotics kits to satisfy their interests. The same can be said for coding and other computer-related pastimes. Confused about how to get started? Try checking out the offerings at your neighborhood library, community center, or community college for some introductory classes.

Remember that aimlessly browsing social media sites like Facebook and Twitter isn't the most productive way to spend your time online. Learn web development or other technical skills that will keep your mind active and stimulated.

Why Having a Hobby Is Important

In today's fast-paced world, it's rare to find an opportunity to relax and reflect. There is so much on the agenda that carving out leisure time seems impossible.

A person's life can gain new meaning and purpose when they discover an interest outside of their professional sphere. What do you want most in the world when you're under the most pressure? Finding something you enjoy doing that allows you to relax and have fun in your spare time is well worth the time and effort it takes to do so. Find a hobby that you enjoy and that enhances your life if you lack inspiration and motivation in your daily routine.

Doing what you love takes away all your worries and stresses. This is your time to be alone and concentrate on yourself without interruption. The mental and emotional benefits of being in this state are immense. Because in the end, all you want is to be happy, relaxed, and present, it's crucial to have a hobby, whether it's an indoor or outdoor activity.

Of course, working can help you build your resume and your bank account, but if you're not getting the fuel you need to keep going, all that effort will be for naught. A short vacation, mental reset, or even a small amount of forbidden pleasure is all that is required. Adding a new interest can improve your life in many ways, from your work to your relationships. Therefore, a reasonable middle ground can be found.

What Role Do Hobbies Play in a Healthy Lifestyle?

Typically, we think of life as nothing more than the necessary evils of making a living, keeping friends, and paying bills. But the truth is that you need time for yourself if you want to live a full life, a time in which you can rest, rejuvenate, and rediscover your motivation.

Do you still have doubts about engaging in a relaxing activity? Then keep reading to find out how beneficial it can be to divert your attention away from your problems and into a hobby.

Aids in Making New Friends

When individuals discover that they have a common interest in a new area, a new bond is formed. Recreational activities can be a great way to break the ice and get to know someone. When two people have a lot in common outside of their formal relationship, it can flourish very quickly. Why? Connecting with others who have similar passions and interests can help break down barriers to communication and understanding. Taking up painting as a hobby is an excellent way to meet new people and expand your social circle.

Motivation from others is invaluable when learning new skills or exploring new interests. As a result, you are more likely to try new things and push past your comfort zones. How exciting does that sound to you?

Helps you avoid developing unhealthy routines.

If you want to avoid the destructive effects of boredom and gain more free time, finding a hobby or pastime can help. Many of the problems that plague our modern society can be traced back to a lack of stimulation, or boredom. This is because when one is idle, negative thoughts dominate their consciousness, making them more vulnerable to engaging in potentially harmful activities like excessive drinking, gambling, or drug use.

The ability to spend time doing something you find rewarding is a major perk of having a hobby. Instead of mindlessly scrolling through social media or channel surfing on your phone, rediscovering your favorite pastime is a surefire way to beat boredom and provide a welcome diversion from the stresses of everyday life.

Build Your Self-Esteem

Overcoming adversity is a great way to bolster pride and confidence in oneself. Taking up a new hobby can help you become more skilled and resilient in other areas of your life. You may be wondering at this point how engaging in something enjoyable could help you get out of a sticky situation.

To sum up, then, any pastime is an opportunity to practice and perfect that ability. For example, if you're passionate about football and have only recently started playing, you'll continue to improve and will soon be able to compete at a very high level. When you make steady progress, you gain a sense of satisfaction that helps you see the benefits of your efforts and encourages you to keep working hard until you achieve your goal.

Unleash Your Imagination

Feeling nostalgic for your childhood, when you could freely decorate your room with whatever you wanted to paint? You can expect to continue to enjoy drawing, sketching, and painting as an adult if you did so during your formative years. It's an indicator of your natural inventiveness, which can be honed with consistent effort.

Of course, there are exceptions to this rule. Do you think of yourself as someone who lacks artistic ability? If you're having trouble letting your imagination run free, it might help to try out a few different hobbies. You won't know how creative you really are until that time comes.

Excellent for Avoiding Mood Swings

It's not easy to juggle work, family, and other commitments. With work, picking up the kids from school, and meeting deadlines, life can feel like it's squeezing you between a rock and a hard place at times. When you have a lot on your plate, adding a new hobby can feel like a lot of extra work. Taking part in it will energize, fulfill, and delight you.

When dealing with depression, it can be helpful to take your mind off of things and focus on something else. Not everyone needs to leave the house to have a good time; staying in and doing things like reading, knitting, or playing with pets can be just as rewarding. Think about the activities you enjoy doing regularly or at least once a week, and make time to do them. It's only over time that people will begin to see the benefits.

Advantages of Physical Fitness

To enjoy the positive effects on health, it is not necessary to partake in an extremely strenuous activity. In addition to improving your health and mood, engaging in pleasurable pursuits can lower your stress levels and blood pressure.

The motivation to start working out is high at first, but after a few days, it becomes a chore and the person gives up on their goals of muscle toning, weight loss, or stomach flattening. Activities that get you moving, like jogging, kayaking, hiking, and dancing, not only help you de-stress mentally and emotionally but also have physical benefits like lowering your body fat percentage and boosting your bone density. Therefore, the next time you indulge in your pastime of choice in the comfort of your own home, keep in mind that you are still contributing to your psychological and physiological well-being.

Find a Hobby When Nothing Interests You

In all honesty, a lack of interest is very common and something that many of us may experience at some point in our lives.

We think it's important to not stifle the chance for introspection, especially if you're showing signs of disinterest, demotivation, or even a lack of ambition. We believe it is important to not suppress boredom when it arises because it can actually inspire creativity and new ways of thinking.

On a related note, many people believe that today's youth are not given enough time to unwind and be themselves because there is always something demanding their attention. This leaves them feeling disjointed and disoriented whenever they find themselves with some free time.

In addition, if you subscribe to some of the stoic philosophy, you may want to actively seek out such times when you feel completely bored and uninterested because it may often disclose vital life lessons.

With this newfound knowledge, I hope you'll be able to see that indifference isn't always a bad thing, but rather a path to new ideas and, who knows, maybe even a new hobby.

Justifying your boredom and finding constructive ways to deal with it will make the feeling of boredom less intimidating.

This post will help you not only find new things that pique your interest but also understand why you aren't as captivated by others. This is because we will be delving deeper into some of these techniques and frames of mind.

Given the foregoing, we'll look into six approaches and measures you can take to develop an interest in something when you have none.

Find a Hobby When Nothing Interests You

One's hobby is something one like to do in their spare time. People engage in this activity in their spare time because they enjoy it or have a natural talent for it.

"Boredom" refers to a mental state characterized by a lack of interest, motivation, and aspiration. However, this may be because some regions of the brain are dormant during boring tasks, leading us to believe that stimulating these regions is the most effective strategy for warding off boredom. However, if these regions aren't healthy, it may be harder than we imagine to rediscover a passion for something.

There is a widespread feeling of boredom. Since we've evolved to prioritize pleasure over pain, boredom ranks high on the list of mental anguish that can be experienced. Some of the many causes of monotony include a lack of drive, interest, or challenge, or an overload of familiarity. It usually happens when we have to wait for something or someone.

During these times, it can be beneficial to take up a pastime that reignites a dormant interest or passion, giving us the push we need to get back to doing what we once enjoyed. Try going for a swim during your lunch break if you're having trouble concentrating at work due to boredom.

You probably understand what it's like to be overwhelmed by a ton of work or to be too tired to give a hoot about anything. Instead of trying to come up with new ideas and motivation, it's easier to just get things done. The trouble is this disinterest and apathy are unlikely to last as long as you'd like. Feeling like your own willpower is the only thing that can get you back on track is discouraging enough; knowing that's not the case makes things that much more discouraging.

In some situations, everyone is open to the same kinds of manipulation. Anxiety, exhaustion, and mental illness are all possible precipitating factors. It's easy to dismiss the idea that a little boredom could be helpful, but the truth is that it can help you focus on what's truly important in life when you're otherwise distracted.

Finding an activity that fascinates you and avoiding boredom

Always pushing yourself to improve is the key to becoming a master of your hobby.

Such situations occur frequently in real life. Despite their years of experience, some programmers may know only one language and have never worked with any other programming paradigm.

Consider your hobby as a long-term decision that will affect every aspect of your life. It's something you should work on refining over time. Eventually, you'll learn enough to be considered an expert. Although it has nothing to do with your actual job, it is something you will use frequently in your personal life.

Trying and failing

Explore a variety of options until you find something that clicks with you. Get into shape by trying out a few different sports at the gym. Get some drawing and painting experience or learn about sculpture. You might not know what you like to do until you try it.

While this plan is simple in concept, some may lack the motivation to put it into action. One way to find inspiration is to think about the things that excite or mean the most to you. If you find yourself at a loss for words, maybe think about why you chose your profession or what you consider to be the most meaningful aspects of your life. Still, struggling to get motivated? Observe people who share your interests; you never know when their enthusiasm might rub off on you.

Consider the onset of the emotion.

The best way to deal with a sudden lack of interest in past activities is to keep track of your feelings and consider when they first appeared. One way to do this is to try to trace back the beginning of your disinterest.

Because it allows us to experience the emotions and mental state we had during that time.

When you take the time to get to know and gain control over your feelings, you can examine why you suddenly decided your hobbies were boring or why you felt like you couldn't find anything that will offer you any inspiration.

As a result, rather than letting your emotions run the show, you will be able to intervene at the moment by using your emotional skills to analyze and reevaluate your train of thought. Doing so will help you maintain control over your emotions.

Is it reasonable that I will always be tired of everything? is a good question to consider asking. And the answer to that is no because it is implausible to think that you will be bored for many years without any significant changes to your environment.

If you employ this strategy, you'll be well on your way to developing healthy coping mechanisms for dealing with boredom. This means that you will be able to let go of critical questions to combat your overwhelming emotions, even if there are times of relative calm.

Return to the beginning

Now that you know how to effectively deal with a loss of interest in past times and activities, we can begin exploring some potential options to help you find a pastime.

The first thing you can do is get back to basics because this will highlight your best qualities and show people what makes you unique.

In other words, if you want to quickly satisfy your need for progress in a new hobby, play to your strengths rather than trying to overcome your weaknesses.

There's no point in trying to change every aspect of who you are if you're already having trouble staying motivated; instead, lean on the strengths that come naturally to you.

If, for example, you have a particularly muscular frame or are otherwise well-developed physically, you might be better off pursuing a hobby connected to physical fitness than a career in physics.

Putting your efforts into areas where you already excel can be very beneficial. However, please understand that this is only meant as a disclaimer and not as an attempt to prevent you from exploring new options.

Make some friends

If you don't have anything that piques your interest, you might not have many friends who will push you to try new things or cheer you up when you're feeling down.

You can put as much or as little effort into making friends as you like, and in the modern world, it's surprisingly easy to communicate with millions of people from all over the world using any of several online discussion boards or social media sites.

Meet New People Here's the handle of a forum where people can talk about making new friends online.

Friends have a way of nudging you out of your comfort zone and into the unknown when you're hanging out with them or talking to them.

You give in anyway because you don't want to disappoint them, but you could end up having a great time doing a variety of things because you accommodated their wishes.

Being the lazy creatures that we are, if given the choice most of us would rather not exert ourselves too much. You get more out of life when you share it with other people and less when you do things alone.

Be a child once again

This may sound strange when you've already seen and done everything, but it's actually a great way to find a new hobby.

There's a greater propensity to try new things and take chances because your brain didn't finish developing until later in childhood.

Because you're discovering so many things you enjoy or want to go out of your way to try, this is also one of the best times of your life. That's why you're living through one of the best times ever.

When we are young, we are more likely to be attracted to things that we can relate to or that make use of our strengths because we rely more on our intuition than on reasoning.

This is a great place to start if you're in search of a new hobby: revisit the activities you enjoyed as a kid, play to your strengths, and trust your instincts if something clicks.

Utilize the tools you have available.

The world is teeming with opportunities just waiting to be seized, but sometimes it isn't so much that you aren't interested in something as it is that you don't know enough about those opportunities to take advantage of them.

To help you reignite the spark that already exists within you, we've compiled a long list of hobbies—more than 300—complete with detailed explanations.

In addition, you'll find a wealth of useful information on our sites, such as guides to specific hobbies, categorized lists of hobbies, and even dedicated sections for certain hobbies, like arts and crafts.

The content presented on our website is just the tip of the iceberg; for a more comprehensive exploration, you can use additional resources like YouTube and other blogs.

The best place to start is with the people closest to you, your own family. You never know what your ancestors enjoyed doing in their spare time when they were younger, let alone what they do now.

Meeting new people is crucial when looking for a new hobby, and it can also help you discover opportunities you weren't aware of before.

Change your negative habits with positive ones.

Overindulging in some form of entertainment, be it a daylong Netflix binge, an evening out with friends, or an excessive number of takeout meals is a perfectly normal occurrence. Even though there are certain necessities for daily functioning, it is also possible to indulge to an unhealthy degree.

Your unfavorable actions may be to blame if you've realized that you lack interest in a wide range of activities.

To determine whether or not these negative habits can be changed, it is sometimes necessary to break them down into their most basic components.

Instead of wasting time watching Netflix all day, you could use that time to learn how to create your own videos or movies. Evidently, you enjoy the media's possibilities and entertainment; as such, you should inform others about this.

Perhaps you enjoy the camaraderie that comes with going out for drinks; if this is the case, rather than ordering a drink as a patron, why not try your hand at mixing one?

It's easy to focus on the wrong thing, which can lead to a detour, but sometimes all that's needed is a little adjustment of direction. It's not always the case that bad habits are the only option.

Push your hand out.

Sometimes the only thing preventing you from achieving greatness or discovering a new hobby is you, and if you don't face that fact sooner in life, you'll never know what might have been.

Do you know how many books there are that offer advice on how to improve your own motivation or bring your dreams to life?

To give you an idea of scale, there are millions, and it's not just books.

Motivating yourself is a skill that can be learned from a variety of sources, including blogs, e-books, paid courses, and YouTube videos.

It is easy to let fear of failure prevent you from trying something new or from pursuing a passion you have long held but have been putting off. Putting obstacles in your path can help you avoid both of these outcomes.

To sum up, anxiety and doubt can be misunderstood for disinterest, but if you admit they're holding you back, you'll have a better grasp on the challenge at hand and the options available to you.

It might require a lot of effort on your part, and it might force you to confront your fears, but once you've done both, you'll be able to put those things in the past.

See a doctor

Something far more serious, like depression, may be to blame for your ability to find things appealing rather than your level of dedication or drive.

If you're having trouble maintaining motivation, finding pleasure, or settling into a routine that works for you, it may be time to schedule an appointment with your primary care physician.

There are usually easy solutions to these sorts of issues that will get you back on track with your hobby quickly.

But sometimes, whether due to our genes or our upbringing,

the deck is stacked against us. It is easy to be critical of oneself when one is surrounded by people who appear to have perfect lives.

Understand stoicism

If you've exhausted our suggestions and are still at a loss, consider taking up the study of stoicism in order to conquer your boredom and discover what you truly enjoy doing in life.

If you're not familiar with the term, here's a textbook definition of stoicism

- The ability to bear suffering or adversity without showing any signs of emotion and without making a complaint

This begs the follow-up question, "Why wouldn't I complain about the pain or difficulties in my life when they actually hurt me?"

We're not saying you shouldn't feel angry or frustrated sometimes, but if these things happen frequently, you need a philosophy that can help you learn to deal with them.

It's possible that you're not destined to excel at anything in particular.

Embracing a stoic lifestyle as a hobby is a great way to express your unique personality, so there's no reason to hide your stoicism.

Notable historical figures who adhered to Stoicism include the great Roman Emperor Marcus Aurelius and the world-famous philosopher Socrates. To this day, Stoicism remains one of the world's most widely studied and practiced philosophical traditions.

Following in their footsteps can lead you to greatness and deeper understanding, both of which may cause you to rethink what initially piqued your interest.

Can You Have Too Many Hobbies?

Yes, but your outcomes will depend on the decisions you make. Even if having a wide variety of interests can help you zero in on the one or two that truly pique your interest, you may not be able to call yourself an expert in any of them if you don't devote time to becoming an expert in any of them. A lot of people struggle to maintain focus on multiple tasks at once.

You'll feel overwhelmed by the mountain of tasks that require your attention but that you haven't had time to complete. Despite this, mainstream culture does not endorse the idea that a person should be interested in many different things. "Jacks of all trades, masters of none" is a common phrase used to describe people who are interested in a wide variety of things but lack expertise in any one area.

But this is only true if you don't give adequate consideration to picking your hobbies. Experts advise that if you want to pursue multiple interests, you should do so across a variety of carefully chosen fields to avoid becoming quickly bored.

How many interests are too many, then?

Reddit's lifehacks subreddit suggests you should focus on no more than three or four areas of interest. That's about as lofty a goal as a healthy human being can take on without burning out.

Maximize your profits if you can do so by turning your unique interests into a source of income.

To start, let's take a look at the problems that arise when you try to pursue multiple hobbies that don't really work for you.

1. There are Way Too Many Options

In theory, having multiple hobbies gives you more flexibility, but in practice, it makes it harder to decide which one will help you achieve your goals.

- Do you game?

- Do you sing?

- Are you capable of becoming the next Picasso?

Even though the options are limited, you will find that you are unable to focus on anything because there are so many things vying for your attention.

2. Zero Specialization

You can't expect to excel in everything you try, but with practice, you can become very good at a few things.

There aren't many athletes who are also accomplished musicians, disc jockeys, or cooks.

At this stage, specialization becomes an option.

Perhaps you're very interested in painting, soccer, and video games, but only one of these will actually make your heart race.

3. The Time Difference

The fact that you can't follow the latest developments in all of your interests if you try to follow several at once is just one more reason why trying to multitask is a bad idea.

As a result, you're constantly spreading your attention thin across a number of different tasks.

Have you ever been so swamped by life that you forgot to watch the season finale of your favorite show on television?

If you've ever been compelled to watch a movie that came out months after you wanted to see it because it interfered with your pursuit of other interests, then you deserve a hearty round of applause.

You know firsthand the time delay that occurs when trying to do too much all at once.

So, You Can Have Multiple Hobbies Sometimes?

I mean, that's the whole point. If you must pick more than four, try to disperse them evenly across the four broad categories.

The 4-hobby rule is an approach to multitasking that helps you give each activity the focus and energy it deserves while reducing the likelihood of friction between them. In order to get the most out of their free time, this rule of thumb advises hobbyists to pick pursuits that involve using all parts of themselves, including their bodies, minds, hearts, and neighborhoods.

1. Physical

Participate in a physically active hobby to improve your health and fitness.

Dancing, hiking, or any other form of physical activity that captures your interest would be fantastic.

One of the best ways to clear your mind and tune into your body is to engage in some sort of physical activity. As a result, they give you the boost you need to accomplish anything else.

2. Cerebral

Your secondary pursuit should be something that encourages positive mental health.

A healthy body is the foundation for a healthy mind.

If your mental health is poor, no amount of effort on your part will bear fruit.

Mental exercises such as crossword puzzles, sudoku, reading, and meditation have been shown to enhance concentration and focus.

3. Creative

The third piece of advice is to find a hobby that stimulates your creativity.

Something like writing, painting, cooking, or singing could fall into this category.

Taking part in creative activities can help you feel more accomplished in life.

Think about how great it will feel when you've reached the pinnacle of your hobby.

4. A focus on community

Your fourth and final interest should focus on giving back to the local community.

You may use it to make the world a better place, or just simply connect with the people in your life.

You may join a local soup kitchen, clean the beach, or join a reading club.

The 4-hobby rule, as you can see, eliminates the boredom problem, and mitigates the effects of the first disadvantage ('too many options).

What Happens If I Can't Adhere to the 4-Hobby Rule?

There's no point in forcing yourself to stick to the 4-hobby rule if you've already exhausted all four options.

With some creative application, you might be able to narrow your interests down to a manageable group of three or four pursuits, even if you do repeat yourself.

Invest time in pursuits that contribute to your development in all facets of your being.

If you find yourself unable to follow the 4-hobby rule, I suggest you investigate the following options:

- Languages

- Music

- Traveling

- Art

- Culinary (can be baking)

- Good mental health (can be exercise, yoga, or meditation)

Take in a new bit of knowledge each and every day (anything from physics to accountancy) Choose a few that pique your interest and give yourself some time to zero in on just one or two.

How Should Hobbies Be Prioritized?

Even the most well-organized among us are prone to making a mess of things now and then.

Whether or not you follow the "four-hobby rule," these principles can help you prioritize your interests.

1. Eliminate clutter.

The human mind is restless, always looking for something new to learn. These days, one must first learn to tune out the world's constant barrage of distractions.

2. Monitor and tweak

Continue monitoring your progress and adjusting as necessary.

3. Try, look, and shuffle

If you want to succeed, you can't afford to repeat the same moves. Discover what you're good at by trying new things, and then commit to doing that.

What Should You Do If Your Interest Is No Longer Fun?

One possible effect of aging is a loss of enthusiasm for formerly enjoyable pursuits.

There isn't much time for hobbies or socializing, and you rarely leave the house. When this happens, it's normal to feel uninspired and bored. If that's the case, what should you do?

After a while, people usually stop caring about the things they used to enjoy doing.

Thankfully, the situation isn't as dire as it seems. The pleasure you once felt when engaging in your preferred activities can be rediscovered in a number of different ways. Meeting new people, joining a club, or trying out new things are all good examples.

While waiting for the bus or having free time at home, you could use your phone to play games or check social media. Definitely, these are wonderful ways to kill time. Still, we can't call them hobbies if you only do them to pass the time.

A deflationary decline in your interest in past times may result from the following explanations.

1. Viewing it as a Dangerous Sport

Without even realizing it, we have turned our hobbies into competitive sports.

Thus, we were able to end any pleasure we may have derived from it.

Some people are hit so hard by it that they burn out and sometimes never recover.

Many people today appear to care only about their own personal success in their chosen fields.

When people do this, they compare themselves to others who have the same interests.

If you're doing something only for the sake of success and not because you enjoy it, you'll eventually get bored of it.

Your hobby will become more of a chore if you force yourself to compete with other people.

2. Aiming for Perfection

The good and bad results of social media are both widely recognized. That caused some people to stop participating in those activities altogether. The results, however, are something you end up disliking.

Because of this setback, you surrender and give up. Having this attitude makes any effort to improve your abilities futile.

Even if you think something has the potential to work out in the long run, you can never fully commit to it. We see your point, but the pursuit of perfection traps its victims. When our plans fail, it's easy to start doubting our abilities and convincing ourselves that we're not cut out for that particular task. This planet, however, is not without its problems. If your pursuit of perfection is causing you mental anguish, stop it.

3. We Get Bored Easily

If a person's interest in a hobby begins to wane, it's possible that they will abandon it altogether.

Take a deep breath and think about giving something new a shot if you count yourself among them. You don't have to do any kind of sleuthing to find what you're looking for.

4. We Don't Have the Time

In this fast-paced world, most people's daily routines consist of going to work, sleeping, and going to bed again.

It can be challenging to make time for your favorite activities when your schedule is already packed. But try to find a happy medium.

The risk of burnout increases the more work you have on your plate, so it's important to take breaks even if you're overwhelmed.

Don't be the type of person who is always looking for a way out.

Many of us feel helpless because we don't have enough time, money, or connections to get where we need to go.

These are not valid excuses for ignoring our pursuits.

When Hobbies Become Unfun, There Are Four Things You Can Do

Losing passion for past interests is a common occurrence. The good news is that you have a number of opportunities to reconnect with your interests and find your life's true calling.

1. Recognizing the difference between avoidance and loss of interest

It's common for people to mix up these ideas despite their

differences. This highlights the importance of being able to differentiate between the two.

When you're feeling unmotivated, it's important to determine whether you've lost interest in the activity or if you just have very negative thoughts about it.

If you find yourself in the second category, it may be time to try something new or seek professional help because you may have formed unfavorable associations with the activity.

2. Get a friend or mentor, or sign up for a group

When you work with a companion who shares your interest, you can quickly rediscover the joy you once felt for the activity.

If you've lost interest in the topic and are having trouble getting back into the swing of things, enrolling in a class, or joining a group may help. Taking part in a group or course is a fantastic way to expand your knowledge and network with people who share your passions.

3. Discover the origins of your first passion for the hobby.

You can get back into doing something you used to enjoy if you can remember why you liked it so much in the first place. If you're not sure about the activity, try a less complicated version.

Even if you've lost interest in the kitchen, you can take baby steps toward rekindling your passion for baking. You can use pancake mix instead of a chocolate cake recipe and save yourself a lot of time and effort. The joy and fervor you once felt for your interest will return once you do this.

4. Pick up a new hobby

If you find that none of the preceding solutions work, you may want to try something different. Create a list of things that might interest you, and pick one.

The next step is to learn more about the topic and decide if it actually interests you. Know that you can't tell if a hobby is right for you until you give it a try. It's natural to lose interest in some past passions. However, there are paths to rekindling your passions. Although it could take some time, you will eventually be successful. A person who does not already have a hobby can always develop.

Is it a hobby, an interest, or just a pastime?

How do you spend your time when you're not working?

When you're housebound, wide awake, or waiting for the bus, and you have a few minutes to kill?

Maybe you're occupying yourself with something like Candy Crush, or Facebook, or just staring aimlessly out the window.

Consider asking yourself, "Do I really appreciate doing those things?" Do you feel satisfied after using them?

Most of the time, saying "no" is the best option when responding to this question.

After realizing what I'm doing, the next logical question is, "Why?"

Neither entertaining nor interesting, the events fall short. Why spend your time with them if you could be doing something else instead?

Idleness on my part.

These are not hobbies because no matter how much time you devote to them, they are not enjoyable to you. The act of watching TV, surfing the web, or playing a video game helps you unwind and relieve stress.

But the truth is that anything along these lines can be considered a hobby. The criteria for hobbies and interests are not met by these pursuits.

When you encounter a curiosity, it piques your interest. You're eager to learn as much as possible about them, and you don't mind spending a lot of time doing so.

Indulging in media like films, books, and podcasts can help you learn more about subjects that interest you. Though math and zoology may pique your interest, they aren't really hobbies. An interest is different from a hobby. A hobby is something that you do simply because you enjoy it. You're itching to get started on them. As a result of engaging in your hobby, you develop and hone a wide range of skills.

Next, we must ask: what is the difference between an interest and a hobby? Hobbies are the activities that one enjoys engaging in when one has free time. The opposite is true of things that pique your interest. Since when have you last had something like that? Do you remember when your parents put you in after-school programs? That is, unless you've never been interested in anything. Perhaps you've always felt like you were born without the "hobby gene."

Sometimes I feel like I'm not accomplishing much in life. Honestly, I wouldn't say that I'm the worst student ever. My current position is not ideal, but it pays well. I do a respectable job, but I'm not the best there is. My outcomes aren't great but not terrible, either. Everything about me, including my skills, feels like a failure.

I know it's unrealistic to expect perfection from oneself and that it's fine to be "average" in some areas so long as you excel in others. In spite of this, I never feel like I've made it. Everywhere you look, all you'll find is mediocrity. I've been putting off getting a steady job because I'm afraid I'll have to accept something less than perfect. I worry that I'll never be anything more than a mediocre person

What are you good at?

The term "mediocre" refers to something that is just average in quality. Half of any given population is, by definition, above average, and the other half is, by definition, below average. This is true of every group of people. Considering it this way, there is nothing wrong with being a below-average performer in most or even all aspects of life. Finding those one or two areas where you really excel is the challenge.

Just like every other person on Earth, you have some special talent of your own. How to find yours in the wild:

1. Give in to your curiosity.

You've probably heard the advice "follow your passion" a million times, but I don't think it's very good. My advice is to instead give in to your inherent inclination toward inquisitiveness. You can do this simply by being aware of what interests you and holds your focus as you go about your daily life. When you're surfing the web or using a social media platform, what catches your eye? What tasks do you perform at work or school that you find yourself most looking forward to? These seemingly insignificant occurrences are, in fact, clues that will lead you to the topics that most pique your interest.

In order to avoid feelings of dissatisfaction and settle for nothing less than excellence, it is crucial to remember that these goals require more than merely engaging in a pursuit one enjoys. The secret to a happy and fulfilling life is finding the activity that combines all three of these factors: what you're good at, what you enjoy doing, and what the rest of the world values.

In order to learn what you enjoy doing, try your hand at many different activities. It's possible that the things you enjoy and excel at the most will have nothing to do with the ideal version of yourself you've always imagined. Purposefully explore different fields until you find the one that best suits your needs, complements your abilities, and allows you to reach your full potential.

2. Push yourself to work hard.

Early on in my life, I realized there are a lot of people who are smarter than me with regards to different things. Because of this, I often felt like I was being treated unfairly because I had to work so much harder than anyone else to achieve the same results. Now, I get to rejoice in all of that hard effort. My professional achievements can be attributed more to hard work than to any innate abilities I may possess.

Yet, practice and hard work are required of everyone, not just those who are born with a natural aptitude. For instance, in his best-selling book Outliers, Malcolm Gladwell shows how exceptionally gifted musicians, software engineers, and other professionals achieved their success by working ten times as hard as their contemporaries. When I think about the people who have made it big in the world, whether as business owners, community leaders, authors, or performers, I realize that they have all put in a lot of work. The lesson to be learned from this is that shortcuts are never guaranteed.

Try not to lose your cool as this process continues. Having well-defined targets to aim for can help you focus your efforts and make progress. Discovering a community of people who share your goals is a huge boost to your progress. For the upcoming year, you may decide to improve yourself by studying something new. As such, you may want to consider becoming a part of a group that can serve as a resource for you as you work to develop and hone your skill.

Why You're Not as Successful as You Could Be

Today has been one of those days in which nothing goes right. Let's be honest: it's a terrible ordeal from start to finish. There are some things that can happen, like the power going out on your block, that is completely out of your control, and as a result, you might not be as productive as you could be. On the other hand, you could be holding yourself back for any one of the twenty-five reasons mentioned earlier.

1. You're lazy

This is the main reason why most people don't succeed in what they set out to do, says author Jim Kukri. In addition, "Every single successful person puts in a tremendous amount of effort in order to achieve their goals. If you want to be lazy, that's OK with me. Just acknowledge it. However, you are not allowed to complain about your lack of wealth and success, okay?"

2. You keep asking "Why not me?"

Like whining, wasting time by trying to figure out why some people have success while you haven't is pointless. In most cases, it wasn't because of a lucky lottery ticket or a wealthy ancestor. Everyone who has ever lived has experienced it, is currently experiencing it, or will at some point in the future. As a human being, you will face challenges, but they will never be the same for any two people. Perhaps you've finally arrived at your moment. As opposed to moping about it, you should make a change that will help you break out of your rut and find success.

3. You become mentally stuck

You'll notice that there are commonalities among successful people. They took the next step toward realizing their dreams. Instead of daydreaming and worrying about everything that could go wrong, they start working on the dream and creating the foundation. It has been said that legendary NHL player Wayne Gretzky once said, "You miss 100% of the shots you never take." Feel free to test it out.

4. Social media is taking up too much of your time

Did you know the average American checks their Facebook, Twitter, and other social media accounts a whopping 17 times a day? Although I understand the importance of maintaining connections with clients and other opinion leaders, I urge you not to devote all of your free time to social media. According to my findings, the most efficient time of day to connect with friends and family is in the evening, after the day's stresses have subsided a bit and there is less to do. This includes reading the news and articles first thing in the morning, which takes only a few minutes. Set aside a specific amount of time for each of these tasks, and stick to it.

5. You never complete what you begin

Many wise people throughout time have said, "Starting is simple, but completing is hard." Having patience and sticking with a task until the end is important, but so is knowing when to give up and throw in the towel. Don't expect overnight results; anything worthwhile is going to take time and effort on your part.

6. You lack the business mindset

Whether you're a freelance writer or the owner of an online store selling basketball shoes, you will never be successful if you treat your work like it has nothing in common with a real business. If you need this money, it's a real business, and you should start treating it like any other 9-to-5 job.

7. You don't have confidence in yourself

If you don't have faith in yourself, how can you say you're willing to put forth the effort necessary to achieve success? You need to find ways to boost your self-assurance, even if that means recognizing and applauding relatively inconsequential wins, like securing a potential client's contact details. Enjoy the fruits of your success, no matter how small. Don't lowball yourself, either to others or to yourself. As with anything else, one's self-esteem should rise in proportion to one's efforts in that direction.

8. You think you deserve it

You are not owed anything. It's up to you to put in the work to get what you want out of life. If you tell yourself that you deserve good things, you may procrastinate and miss out on opportunities. Make it happen.

9. You obsess about unimportant things.

I'm not saying you shouldn't have anything to do with your time outside of work, but it's a problem if you're more concerned with finding out if Beyoncé's "Lemonade" will be available to stream on iTunes than you are with following up on a lead that could lead to a paycheck.

10 You refuse to leave your comfort zone

You can feel most at ease and confident when you're doing something within your comfort zone. Sure, there are times when you should be safe and secure, but staying there for too long can cause boredom and even dread, even if it was necessary at the time. It's impossible to grow and improve if you never leave where you are.

11. You could be more productive

Simply working hard for eight hours a day won't ensure success. As a result of things like distractions, breaks, and prolonged concentration on a single task, you might only be able to put in a few solid hours of work each day. It is possible to learn how productive your days actually are by investing in time management and monitoring technologies.

12. You place too much stress on money

Starting a business with the sole expectation that you will become a billionaire is a recipe for disaster. The most prosperous business owners and leaders don't place an excessive emphasis on financial gain. They have set their sights squarely on creating a superior end result. If you find your true calling, as the old adage goes, you'll never have to work another day in your life.

13. You're not passionate

If you don't enjoy your work, even if it requires 100% of your effort, you'll only give it 50% of your attention. You won't be able to keep your enthusiasm and drive going without passion, especially when times get tough.

14. You think negatively

Without even trying, a pessimist or someone prone to negative thinking will ruin their chances of success. You're setting yourself up for failure, to put it another way. Try to improve your outlook on life by increasing your awareness of your surroundings and spending time with upbeat people. Watch the internal dialogue you have with yourself. Self-talk. Notice if you tend to spend most of your time venting your frustrations to other people in conversation. You may want to try something different if that describes the majority of your interactions.

15. You don't have any goals set.

You never seem to have any kind of plan in place. Somehow, you've come to believe that if you just wish hard enough, your desires will come true. That's not how the system works. Set goals for yourself and work hard to realize them. If you aren't a big planner or list-maker, that's fine. Becoming a small-scale planner and list-maker is an excellent place to begin. Taking things one step at a time and concentrating on a single component of the list is all that is required.

16. You don't know who you are

Thus, it is important to reflect on and capitalize on your unique set of skills and strengths. You should also know what you value and set reasonable goals for yourself. The first step in accomplishing anything is to find your true identity. Tell me about your preferences. Rectify your lack of focus

17. You don't fight hard enough to win

Sometimes we wish we could just throw away our lives and start over. The feeling may disappear after a day or linger for weeks. To sum up, success is not automatic; it requires work. This is an integral part of the procedure. The fact that you're having trouble achieving your goals at the moment is not a good enough reason to give up on them forever. Don't rush things.

18. You believe you can do it all on your own

Most people think that successful businesses were all started by lone individuals. It couldn't be further from the truth. Wozniak, Allen, and Saverin played critical roles in the development of the companies founded by Jobs, Gates, and Zuckerberg. Think about it like this: even if you're an expert builder, how far could you get in constructing your own home if you did everything by yourself? You will still need the help of others, such as a plumber or an electrician, to complete the building project, no matter how skilled or experienced you are. The most you have to lose is a friend along the way. You should immediately begin working on creating one for yourself if you do not already possess one.

19 You haven't done a good job at financial management.

Poor financial management is a leading cause of a small business's demise. But if you let it, this could become an issue even in your personal life. Spending more than you earn makes it impossible to save for emergencies or retirement. Make a plan for your money and stick to it. Consult with a financial advisor if you feel that you need to. It's possible to get free advice on budgeting and other money matters in a number of different cities. Programming for adults is also available, though at a significantly reduced rate. One of the first things you should do is make a running total of all of your regular outgoing costs and keep that number front and center at all times. Its okay to eat a can of soup at home instead of going out to a fancy restaurant every once in a while.

20. You strive for constant perfection

That's not an excuse to hand in mediocre work. It implies that you shouldn't waste your time trying to perfect things, but rather on actually doing them, such as accomplishing your goals. Keeping your efforts consistent and putting one foot in front of the other daily can help you get where you want to go. Also, setting a time limit can help you focus on getting the best possible result before declaring victory and moving on.

21. You have an inadequate perspective

Don't put all your eggs in the near-term basket. You need long-term goals that will keep you motivated and inspired for decades to come. Tell me about a time when you wished you could do something but didn't. It's best to start practicing the violin now if you're 45 years old and want to learn how to play.

23. You don't seek out new information regularly

Successful people are always looking to better themselves by learning something new or honing an existing skill. You shouldn't turn down opportunities that could help you grow as a person. Reading a book or joining a webinar are two examples of this kind of activity. One of the best ways to keep learning is, in my opinion, simply to be curious about what other people are up to. At least one area of expertise exists in every person. You can learn a lot in a short amount of time from that expert. It's possible that this could also lead to people becoming close friends with one another. At times, you just have to stare your fears in the face.

24. You have no networking skills

Networking is one of the most effective ways to increase your chances of being successful, and it can be done in a variety of settings, including in-person get-togethers, online discussions with prominent figures in your field, and even in-person events. If an influencer tweets a link to an article you just published on your blog, for instance, you'll get exposure that doesn't cost you a dime, which could lead to more people learning about your business and potentially generating new leads. Become a person who can bring people together and who encourages the involvement of everyone. Do not be the type of person who judges others harshly because of their differences. One never knows when one will be the one in need of assistance or when one will be the one to provide assistance to another. It's possible to learn something new when you put yourself in contact with different people.

25. You can't tell when to give up

To reiterate what I've already told you, please don't quit this too soon. However, the ability to let go is an essential skill, so you must know when it's the right time. The ability to let go and move on to new challenges does not imply amnesia for the past.

How to develop expertise in anything

A person who has attained a high level of expertise in a particular field and is looked to for direction and explanations. To be an "expert" in most fields, however, does not necessitate completing any formalized training or examination. For some careers, the "10,000-hour rule" may not be relevant. She says "how hard you work at it" and "your innate abilities" are the two most important factors. Putting in more hours isn't always the answer to getting what you want out of life.

Identify what you know right now

This may seem like a no-brainer, but in reality, many of us have to balance multiple commitments both at work and at home. At home or at the office, it's easy to quickly fill our time with routine, necessary tasks. But before you go any further, there's a very important (and revealing) question you should ask yourself: What is it that you're naturally good at? My advice is to zero in on a skill set that either comes naturally to you or that you enjoy cultivating. Don't forget that there is a customer base for any product. A woman who made millions from selling Scottish Terrier figurines online is one of the most fascinating people I've ever met. Online markets exist for a wide variety of skills, including writing and native language.

Make sure you're passionate about it

If you're going to invest 10,000 hours, a year, or more into training, you should at least enjoy it. Your chances of reaching the top are diminished without enthusiasm, which motivates you to train hard and makes you progress more slowly. While obstacles may arise along the way, "the reason you are on the expert's trip needs to be powerful enough to urge you ahead," she says. "Time spent studying is never wasted" if you can "develop a 'why' that links your learning to a highly desirable conclusion."

Learn to say no and mean it

You can't dominate a niche market by learning the ins and outs of a dozen different industries. Expertise training typically occurs at a time when most of us are already overextended, forcing us to reprioritize our responsibilities. If you want to take Stahl at his word and learn something new in a year, you need to get good at saying "no."

She continues by stating that opportunities are a major distraction, and that not every good one is meant for you. Take care to focus intently on just one task at a time; research shows that switching between multiple tasks at once reduces productivity. Just focus on one thing and master it thoroughly.

Honestly intend your delivery

Getting good at something isn't easy, and no one ever promised otherwise. Therefore, it is essential to make plans for your future development, read materials, and absorb the knowledge of best practices. Stahl suggests the following events as candidates for the year's most memorable moments:

Studying can be done in a variety of ways, including reading, watching films, going to training, talking to experts, and taking online courses.

Stahl contends that becoming an expert requires more than just hard work; you also have to be proud of your achievements and flaunt them. In order to disseminate your expertise, you should start a blog, write for scholarly publications, or make a video blog.

Accept that you will be the big fish in the small pond.

According to Stahl, when we consider being recognized as experts, we typically see ourselves competing with the finest in the world. It would be wonderful if that were the case, but in reality, it's not. Your pond may not always be a literal body of water but rather a physical region or virtual realm. And whether you're catching a few hundred or a few thousand, you'll be regarded as a local expert no matter how deep the water.

You may become an established expert by simplifying complex issues, sharing your knowledge with others, and actively contributing to your field or community.

Having to explain something to someone else is the best method to make sure you understand it yourself. "Since you work in your industry, you already know more than the ordinary individual," Stahl explains. "Your knowledge will increase over time if you are sincere and take the time to study, prepare, and offer a class based on what you know. Very soon, you will be seen as an expert in your field.

When there are too many to choose from

I enjoy playing the piano, drawing, knitting, baking, skating, swimming, dancing, cooking, reading, writing, doing it myself (DIY), learning new languages, scrapbooking, and practicing Karate.

I had a lot of hobbies and pursuits I wanted to engage in but was unable to because of time and money constraints.

I was paralyzed by choice and could not move forward. It was difficult for me to decide on a pastime. After giving it some thought, I decided not to pursue any interest.

Most people, I imagine, have felt the burden of having too many choices, especially when deciding how to spend their free time.

Given that following your bliss is supposed to involve using your own free will, please explain how it is possible that this is the case.

When there are too many options, it can be difficult to decide what to pursue. It can be overwhelming, leading us to waste time and effort deliberating over which interest to pursue, only to find that another interest was more satisfying in the end.

This could make it so that we can't stick with any one hobby for very long and have to keep switching them up. Thus, it is highly unlikely that any of us will ever become experts in any one field.

To become an expert in anything, though, we need to devote a lot of time and energy, but that investment is multiplied when we can narrow our focus to just a few interests. We've decided to focus on becoming experts in a select few hobbies rather than dabbling in many.

What To Do If You Are Attracted to Many Different Interests

There appears to be a plethora of options for doing almost anything today, whether it be for profit, for fun, for entertainment, for academic study, etc.

Unfortunately, our brains weren't built to process such a wide variety of alternatives. The sheer magnitude of the problem often paralyzes us into inaction. It's easy to blame things like laziness, lack of discipline, or lack of enthusiasm when we don't follow through. The abundance of choices is to blame. Because of the overwhelming number of potential outcomes, we become paralyzed and unable to take any action.

It's undeniably beneficial to be able to pursue our individual goals with greater freedom. We live in a world where more choice does not necessarily mean better outcomes. Research has shown that people tend to buckle under the pressure of having too many options. Six different jams were provided as samples to the study participants, with 30% of the participants deciding to purchase a jar. Yet only 3% of the sample population exposed to all 24 jams ultimately bought one. Having to make too many choices can be mentally draining. Too many options practically guarantee that we will do nothing.

People are often paralyzed by the sheer volume of options available to them when trying to make a decision about something as seemingly simple as a hobby or pastime. Many young people as a result give up hope and become directionless in their careers. Whether you're interested in engineering, the arts, physics, economics, mathematics, or computer science, there's a field for you. They are limited to pursuing one interest at a time. They are required to choose a career path by the time they are twenty and remain in it until they reach retirement age.

But what if your enthusiasm for each of these things is equal? Skills (such as writing, coaching, public speaking, art, music, design, engineering, dance, cooking, programming, business, etc.) What should you do if you feel torn between so many interests?

When faced with too many professional options and the pressure to choose the "best" one, many people make the wrong choice and end up worse off. Many others are still on the fence because they don't want to be alone or find out there are better options.

How can we possibly choose a career path from among all these possibilities that will make us happy and fulfilled? But suppose you have multiple areas of curiosity that you'd like to investigate.

In other words, you can find the solution. That's just how things work out: indulge in as many pastimes as you like, provided you don't act like a donkey.

Be human, not a donkey

There's a good chance you're familiar with the legend, but in case you aren't, here's a quick rundown:

The Burden donkey is situated between a stack of hay and a pail of water. There's hay on the left and water on the right, and he can't make up his mind which one to look at. Could you provide some hay and some water? He is unable to make a decision, and as a result, he collapses from hunger and thirst and dies. A donkey can't see very far into the future. It would be more convenient for him to get water before hay.

Every once in a while, we're all faced with the difficult decision of picking one option out of a few that are all equally good. Similar to the donkey, we tend to stand in the middle of the road and mull over our options before making a decision.

In our minds, there is no going back once we've committed to a course of action. We don't actually enter any of them; rather, we just stand there and take a look around.

We can accomplish a lot and delve deeply into many different areas of interest if we don't try to do everything at once.

The lesson here is simple: don't be a jackass. It's about ditching the mentality that says your goals are impossible if you don't complete them all this week.

Just as it's a mistake to think you have to devote your entire life to a single endeavor, it's also a mistake to think you can get everything done in a single burst.

The trick is to take a step back and examine the entire picture. Get set for a long haul. Accept the possibility that you will devote a few years to one goal, another few years to a different one, and so on.

And it's easy to see that Derek puts his own advice into practice. In addition to being an author/publisher and TED speaker, he has worked as an entrepreneur and in the circus. He didn't consciously set out to find or develop those qualities overnight, though.

It's to your benefit to have a wide range of interests and abilities.

Being a man or woman of many interests was once seen as a negative trait, but that opinion has since changed. But in today's interconnected world, this is very quickly becoming a huge boon. Multiple studies have discovered a positive correlation between having a wide range of interests and attaining success.

The current state of the information economy has caused a number of significant changes that are challenging long-held beliefs about the value of specialization. In today's globalized world, people with divergent interests can actually benefit from working together. Being a generalist, as opposed to a specialist, has its advantages.

Knowledgeable experts in many fields, or "polymaths," have made significant contributions to society at large.

One of the most talented people in history is Leonardo da Vinci. Some scholars consider them to be right up there with the brightest minds who have ever lived.

Invention, drawing, painting, sculpture, architecture, science, music, mathematics, engineering, literature, anatomy, geology, astronomy, botany, writing, history, and cartography were only some of the many topics that interested the Renaissance Italian polymath Leonardo da Vinci.

I mean, it's crazy, right?

But there is a catch: he didn't do them all at once.

Countless brilliant minds, such as Galileo, Newton, Aristotle, Franklin, Edison, da Vinci, da Vinci, Curie, Jobs, Feynman, Musk, and many more, spring to mind. Many of the most important people in the past and the present had many different skills and passions.

I can't fathom the motivation behind it.

Their varied academic experiences have equipped them with novel ideas and methods with which to approach problems. Since they can make original inferences, this often results in ground-breaking findings.

To foster a mind that is receptive to new ideas and perspectives, it is beneficial to engage in a wide range of activities and interests. The knowledge you gain in one field can inspire new approaches to solving problems in another.

When compared to the "tunnel vision" that typically characterizes the work of specialists, this is a striking difference. One story can only provide so much context. Focusing on one thing at a time comes with a cost.

If you see yourself as someone with many different passions and aspirations, don't be so hard on yourself. In today's fast-paced global economy, people with your skillset are more in demand than ever before.

The only real obstacle is making the wrong moves as you pursue your interests and develop your abilities.

The door is wide open for you to make a decision. Also, you can adopt a plethora of personas. however, not in a single day.

It would be fantastic to look back and realize that you were proficient in many fields, including but not limited to computer programming, literature, music, engineering, the sciences, photography, and so on.

It could take a few years, or even decades to cycle through numerous hobbies.

Therefore, it is critical to maintain an overarching perspective. Instead of trying to dabble in a dozen different pastimes, focus on just one or two. In a way that allows you to switch gears if you so choose in the future.

You could spend a considerable amount of time pursuing one interest before moving on to another, and so on. But you have to give yourself permission to indulge in a wide variety of pleasures before you can achieve that. And then, even more importantly, you need to develop the persistence, determination, self-control, and focus to focus on a single task for an extended period of time, thereby increasing your chances of becoming an expert in that field.

You can't use the excuse that "I have various hobbies" to waste your life away by constantly changing careers, academic concentrations, and revenue streams.

Most creative insights and breakthroughs require a rare blending of different skills. In addition, in today's ever-shifting environment, those who can financially adapt to a variety of roles are in the best position to do so. Through the exchange of information and ideas, they can create bonds that cannot be made by anyone else and provide access to previously inaccessible knowledge and understanding.

There has been a recent uptick in the number of compliments I've received for the "great ideas" I offer when attempting to resolve a problem. Over the past 15 years, I have dabbled in a wide range of professions and hobbies, including but not limited to teaching, writing, blogging, performing music, giving speeches, photographing, marketing, economics, and even engineering. I take this to mean that people are starting to share their knowledge and skills with one another.

So, if you find yourself interested in many different things, I say, don't be so hard on yourself. Don't act like a moron about it, and you'll realize its benefits.

Do we have too many hobbies?

Step 1: List the top 10 hobbies you are most passionate about.

Don't overwhelm yourself by trying to enumerate every single thing that brings you joy. Since there are so many possibilities, this could prevent any meaningful analysis. Instead, prioritize your top 10 passions.

Step 2: Rank them by increasingly less important details

The next step is to prioritize your interests by ranking them from most important to least. Which activities provide the most excitement for you? Which hobbies do you wish you could start doing right away?

Step 3: Commit to your top two interests

Select two interests. Just the right amount. And make a conscious decision to devote time to such pastimes.

Two hobbies? Here are some questions to ask yourself:

How much of your time do you spend indulging in this pastime for its own sake?

Can you honestly say that you're enjoying yourself while partaking in this pursuit? Or are you partaking in this activity with the hope of gaining social approval?

In other words, how much effort, time, and money will I need to devote to this?

Take into account the resources you have available, the cost, and any specialized gear you may need to pursue that interest. Is there any way you could make time for the hobby in your hectic schedule?

What do you want to accomplish with your leisure pursuits?

Where do you see this hobby taking you? Is it better health, more creative thinking, or higher IQ? Do you just want a casual understanding of your field, or do you aspire to mastery? Just how long do you intend to pursue your passion before finally giving up?

Step 4: Develop Systems

Dedicate a specific day and time to your hobby, and plan as thoroughly as you can.

If you enjoy writing, you can schedule an hour each day at 10 a.m. to do so on your laptop. That's the way your method operates, right?

The next step is to keep going in the same direction.

Do it on a regular basis and make it a habit.

Stay consistent in your behavior.

Step 5: Continue to Improve

Keep improving your abilities after you've established a regular routine for your activity.

If you enjoy writing as a hobby, for instance, you could ask for feedback from readers and use it to improve future works.

The only way to get better at a hobby is to learn from your mistakes.

How to Find a Hobby You'll Stick With

Pursuing an interest is a great way to spend free time. As a means of relieving stress, many individuals turn to hobbies. However, many people find it difficult to keep up with a hobby over time. To find a hobby you can stick with for the long haul, it's important to be practical. Choose an event that works with your time constraints and budget. You should also think about who you are and what you love. When beginning a new hobby, be patient and give yourself time to adjust. If you want to improve your chances of sticking with a new hobby, ease into it.

Making Useful Suggestions

1. **Check your finances.** Some pastimes don't cost nearly as much as others do. Think about your financial situation before settling on a hobby. How much money do you have available?

- Many pursuits call for a wide variety of accessories. Hockey, for instance, is a sport that necessitates specific gear, including a helmet, gloves, a stick, ice skates, and other items. Even if the costs add up quickly, they might be justified if you truly care about the topic.

- If money is tight, think about taking up a hobby that doesn't cost a lot. You only need needles, yarn, and scissors to get started knitting. Although this hobby does require some initial financial outlay, you can find just about everything you need at discount department stores, art supply stores, or even online.

- If your hobby calls for specialized equipment, start small and build up. A $10,000 guitar is overkill for a beginner. It's fine to spend, but first-timers should tread carefully.

2. **Be realistic about your time availability.** You might not enjoy a high-maintenance hobby if you don't have much spare time for it. An activity that takes a long time may seem like a good idea if you have nothing better to do and a lot of free time on your hands.

- Even a short amount of time can be put toward productive pursuits like reading, painting, or solving crossword puzzles. Do it during your lunch break or after the kids are in bed. These can be done in a short amount of time. They might be useful if you're feeling overwhelmed by your commitments.

- A considerable amount of downtime is required for other hobbies. You need to spend some time gardening every day if you want to see results. If you're looking for something to do but have exhausted all other possibilities, this is the activity for you.

3. **Describe your level of sociability.** Be honest with yourself about your need for social interaction. If you're the gregarious type who does better in a group setting, you probably won't stick with an activity that requires you to do it by yourself. If you prefer your own company, you might not have much fun participating in a group activity.

- Joining a sports team or a reading club, for example, might be a great activity if you need the encouragement of others to keep you going.

- Reading, for example, is great for those who like quiet time alone and are more introverted.

Considering Your Tastes and Personality

1. **Consider what makes you happy.** Find something to do that excites and delights you. Don't do your hobby just to impress other people; enjoyment is the whole point. Your long-term results from the activity will suffer if you aren't initially invested in it. Think about the things that fascinate and intrigue you when trying to decide on a hobby.

- Give some thought to the skills you've always wished you had but were never given the opportunity to learn. Do you ever fantasize about making it big as a recording artist? You could potentially enjoy learning to sing in your spare time. Do you ever wish you had the skill to amaze people with your art? Think about grabbing a sketchbook and paints.

- Taking a look back at your life may be really beneficial. Which subject matter did you enjoy learning about the most? Which of your extracurricular activities did you enjoy the most while you were in school? This might help you get insight into the types of interests you could pursue in your adult life.

- Identify your innate abilities. Some people need a hobby that's more relaxing than challenging. Attempting something outside of one's capabilities can raise stress levels, which can make it easier to give up. If you want to do something low-key, consider the abilities you currently possess.

- First and foremost, that's a great step forward if you enjoy preparing your own meals on a nightly basis. You are not a Michelin-starred chef, but you can still put together a tasty meal and are not afraid to experiment in the kitchen.

- Think about taking a cooking class; it could be very beneficial to your career. With your background in cooking, you won't have to learn as many new skills to try out this exciting new hobby.

- Consider how much you enjoy a challenge. It's true that some people lose motivation when developing already-popular skills. If you're the kind of person who gets their kicks out of a good challenge, look for a hobby that will push you to your limits.

- Maybe you're not the party type and prefer a quiet night in. Whether you choose to run or hike, you'll be forced to go outside and get some exercise.

2. **List the things you already find appealing.** Whichever hobby or interest you pursue should say something about you as a person. It's much more likely that you'll stick with a hobby if you pick something that interests you.

- Make a comprehensive list of everything that interests you. Next, examine the record we made. It's time to start thinking about what sort of pastime will best suit your interests.

- Words, literature, language, culture, trivia, and so on are just a few examples of what you could record. In order to comprehend the clues in crossword puzzles, you have to apply your knowledge of trivia and reasoning about words, making them a potentially beneficial activity.

Create a Hobby Stick

1. **Find someone to share your interest with.** Many people think it's best to have a friend nearby when starting a new hobby for the first time. When you and a friend commit to pursuing a new hobby or interest, you both increase your odds of success. You'll be able to keep each other in check.

- Select a pal who shares your passions and values. One of your friends may be into extreme activities, but you'd rather remain home and read.
- Find someone else who shares your passion for books. Maybe you and your friend might join a book club in your area.

2. **Find a neighborhood.** People are more likely to continue with a pastime if they have friends who have an interest in it with them. You could enroll in a class or join a club that focuses on your interest area. If you enjoy singing and would like to share your talent with others, you may want to join a local chorus.

- If you're an introvert, you might benefit from seeking out online support groups. A knitter, for instance, might visit a message board in search of advice and inspiration for a new knitting project.

3. **Begin modestly.** If you dive headfirst into a hobby without enough patience, you risk burning out quickly. Do not feel as though you must immediately and completely commit to your new endeavor. Begin by setting aside some time every day to engage in your hobby. As your skill level in the hobby grows, you should increase this figure.

- If you want to start running, 5 to 10 minutes is a good starting point; as you get in better shape, you can increase the duration of your runs.
- Have patience when trying something new. Learning a new hobby takes time and effort. Be patient with yourself as you work to improve a skill. If you're struggling to keep going, thinking about how you'll benefit from this new skill set can be motivating.

4. **Don't force yourself to keep up a pastime you don't enjoy.** If you never try new things, you'll never know if you like them or not. It's okay if you give a hobby a fair shot but ultimately decide it's not for you. An individual's hobby is a form of recreation practiced in their spare time. If it turns out the opposite is true, you need to keep looking. Remember that you are most likely to keep doing the activity you enjoy the most.

- There's no shame in ditching a hobby that's not enriching your life if you find yourself doing it less and less. It's possible that you'll decide to pursue a different interest in the near future.

When you don't have the money or time

Do you seek a worthwhile hobby that can provide both fun and fulfillment? The benefits of hobbies to one's mental health have been well documented. Plus, they're cheap, if not free. These activities are fun, and many of them don't even require you to leave the house.

The widespread misconception that inexpensive activities are boring is a major factor explaining why so few people partake in them. The truth is that you can have all the excitement, discovery, creativity, self-expression, and joy in the world even on the tightest of budgets. Low-cost activities are not only simple to partake in, but also have the potential to help you rediscover what truly brings you joy in life.

It is not necessary to spend a fortune to have a good time, as there are many enjoyable activities that do not cost anything.

I have a friend who says he has several motorcycles, each of which is several thousand dollars.

Sheesh! Despite the fact that I only spent twenty dollars on a new daypack to use on my travels, I felt like I was going overboard.

If you want to learn how to ride a bike, you can probably find a way to do it without spending a fortune.

Not everyone can afford to participate in every hobby.

So how do you keep your body and mind active without draining your bank account?

Find a cheap hobby, or better yet, pick one of these that won't cost

Hobbies You Can Do for Free

Does the question, "What free hobbies are there?" ever cross your mind? To learn novel approaches to spending leisure time pursuing your interests, read on.

Finding a hobby that is a good fit for your personality can be challenging. Moreover, if you do this, you'll notice that lots of fun things typically cost money. There is a wide variety of hobbies and pastimes out there, including traveling, collecting cars, yacht racing, speedboat racing, skydiving, and many others. This might have you wondering, "What am I able to do for no cost?"

There are plenty of entertaining things you can do without leaving the house that won't cost a fortune. Participating in enjoyable activities reduces stress and improves mental and physical health, according to studies. What's more, you won't even need money to do what you love.

1. Gardening

If you're looking for a free craft that's still exciting, gardening is one of your best bets. Depending on the size of your yard, you might be surprised by the number of edible plants you can find there.

Berry bushes and other wild fruits and vegetables can be found and transplanted into a home garden. By the end, your garden will be brimming with unusual species as well as local flora.

Instead of starting from scratch, tend to the plants you already have. To start over is the other option. Master gardening by tending to low-upkeep flowers and plants.

2. Hiking

Hiking is a fantastic activity for those who wish to spend more time outside. Hiking is a fantastic option for exploring remote regions of the world. You and your pals should get out and discover the nearby landscape, which includes mountains, forests, and water features. It's a lot of fun to learn and even more fun to play well.

You'll feel better than ever before, and the time spent joking around with friends is something you won't soon forget.

3. Meditation

Everyone agrees that meditation is one of the best hobbies you can do from home because it's so easy to get started and has so many positive effects. Beneficial effects on the immune system and anxiety reduction.

In addition to books and articles, audio and video recordings can be a great resource for learning more. Taking a break to meditate is a wonderful way to gain clarity and reconnect with your true self. And everything you could possibly need is already within you.

4. Playing Chess

If you're good at chess, you might enjoy playing a game on the weekend or in the evening with a friend or coworker. Better yet, join a chess club in your area and chat with other chess enthusiasts while sipping coffee.

A recent analysis of the scientific literature suggests that chess isn't just a fun pastime; it can also help you hone skills that can help you succeed in your chosen profession.

It's not necessary to drag out the checkers or chessboard to have a good time. After you've honed your skills, enter tournaments to show off your prowess. I've been playing chess for years, both online and with real people, because it's a lot of fun and really interesting to me (like in the image).

Adding time limits and ratings to a chess game increases the stakes and thrill of the competition. Chess rating improvement is now easier than ever.

5. Bird Watching

Birdwatching is a fascinating hobby that can lead you to all sorts of exciting locations around the world. Becoming a birdwatcher equips you with knowledge about bird behavior, including how each species communicates through its unique calls. Uncommon bird species may be revealed to you.

Keep in mind that almost all bird species prefer rural areas where they can fly freely and safely even if you want to do your birdwatching close to home. Generally speaking, forest regions have a lower population density than the surrounding areas.

6. Photography

An attractive feature of photography is that you need not wait to get started. If you don't already have a great image, you should get one.

Since I value aesthetic harmony in photography, views are my go-to subject. Taking pictures of them is much less challenging than taking pictures of cities or portraits of people.

Start taking your smartphone camera out on evening strolls just before sunset to get used to shooting in low light. I did that for a while because it was soothing. You can find me on Instagram if you're interested in learning how to take better landscape photos with your phone.

After some effort and refinement, photography could become a rewarding hobby that brings in money from the sale of your photos. Check out these photography tutorials on YouTube to hone your craft. The basics of photography, such as aperture, shutter speed, exposure, and ISO, are discussed at length. If you have taken a few good photos and have a grasp of the basics, you can begin making money from your photography.

7. Working out

To the average person who wonders, "What hobbies can I do for free?" the idea of engaging in physical activity probably doesn't immediately come to mind. While exercise may not be everyone's favorite activity, it is one of the healthiest choices you can make. YouTube has many videos that can teach you something or just make you laugh.

You can get a great workout without leaving your house. Mobile devices can be used to watch and follow along with the videos.

Outdoor enthusiasts, however, have the option of evening jogs or sprints around the block. As much as exploring the area on foot might wear you out, it would also be a great way to relax and unwind.

8. Writing A Book

Are you contemplating writing your life story down for others to read? In other words, are you aware that you don't need a publisher to get your work out there?

Write for fun, and you'll be astounded at how much you can do. With just a few hundred words, you can easily self-publish a fantastic text written in your spare time.

9. Personal Care

In the midst of everything going on in our lives, it's easy to lose track of who we are. It's easy to put others' needs before our own when we're not committed to anything. There is no better way to spend free time than on self-care.

Filing her nails, oiling her hair, polishing her shoes, and ironing her clothes are all acceptable ways to make a woman happy. Having a good appearance can do wonders for your self-esteem. Do your best to take care of yourself despite your busy schedule.

Check out how-to videos on how to apply makeup to your face online. It's possible that a change in approach will yield unexpected results. As a result, you'll be able to put that extra time to good use.

10. Fishery

Rather than being a boring way to spend time outdoors, fishing can be quite exciting. A picnic in the woods is the perfect ending to a weekend of fishing. Taking part in this pastime is a wonderful way to spend time with loved ones.

Think of all the excitement you'll have battling with your friends for the few large fish in the tranquil waters. I can only imagine how thrilling this is for you. And you don't need a lot of fancy gear to go fishing. In the nearby waterways, you can cast your rod and reel.

11. Grill

This is your chance to become a master griller in preparation for your next backyard barbecue. Connect with the people who matter to you on a consistent basis.

With practice, you can grill just about anything, from vegetables to meats to whatever else strikes your fancy.

The only things you need to learn how to barbecue are a grill and the food already in your fridge.

12. Watching A Film

You've probably developed a deep affection for a handful of movies that you watch on a regular basis. No longer do you watch films merely for entertainment; instead, you evaluate them on a range of criteria, from the technical aspects of their production to the skill of their actors.

Watching a movie is a fun, inexpensive activity for couples to do together. A date to the movies on a Friday night or Saturday afternoon is always a good time, but it's even more exciting when you and your significant other can talk about what you're seeing and what it means to you.

13. Reading

Reading gives you the opportunity to experience the world through the eyes of another. Reading is great because it can be done anywhere and at any time. Reading for as little as six minutes can reduce stress by as much as 68 percent, so doing so is highly recommended.

Reading can be one of the most relaxing things to do at home when you're feeling tired or stressed. And there's no need for all those books. Visit your local library to borrow your preferred title now.

14. Outdoor Recreation

It's good for you to get some fresh air and natural light. If you're looking for a way to relax after a stressful week, look no further. Camping is a fantastic pastime because it provides a chance to get some fresh air and physical activity away from the rat race of daily life in the city.

A tent, the right shoes, a sleeping bag, and some food and safety supplies are all you need for the best time of your life with your friends in the great outdoors. The next week will be easier to get through now that you're feeling refreshed.

15. Weblogs

Blogging is a fantastic platform for expressing one's opinions and interests on any subject. Writing a blog on WordPress or another free blogging platform can be a rewarding pastime activity.

What makes blogging so engaging is that there is no set schedule or format to adhere to. You can complete this at home if that's more practical.

Do you know that blogging can be a way to earn extra money? Ads, affiliate programs, and product sales are all viable ways to make money off of a blog.

16. Needlework

When I was younger and had fewer responsibilities, I could occasionally ask, "What hobbies can I do for free?" It wasn't long before I was using yarn to create cozy sweaters and socks for infants.

I was the kind to mend my brothers' and sisters' ripped tees and shorts. As a result of my efforts, I was able to enjoy a sense of well-deserved fulfillment.

Needlework is a very satisfying craft activity. When the temperature drops, nothing beats wrapping yourself warm in woolen clothes. The demand for warm accessories like knitted socks, blankets, sweaters, and gloves is on the rise right now.

Making handmade home décor, whether by knitting, crocheting, sewing, or embroidering, is a satisfying hobby. You can make anything out of wool and a needle or a crochet hook.

17. Jewelry Production

Crafting jewelry could be a relaxing and enjoyable pastime. Creating one-of-a-kind jewelry is a wonderful opportunity to impress loved ones with your artistic skills. Once you've mastered this ability, you can use it to make a living.

Creating jewelry can be done in a variety of ways, including with beads or with intricate metalwork. It's a great opportunity to put your creative skills to work while also earning some extra cash online.

Making beautiful jewelry doesn't take much practice to get good at. Several guides on this topic can be found on YouTube.

18. Compose poetry or music

If you find yourself humming along to radio hits, composing your own music could be a great way to express yourself creatively. When I find myself humming along to the lyrics of my favorite artists, it inspires me to write my own.

Several tools that could help you get started could be found here. Using the helpful program Muse Score, you can quickly find yourself working with musicians looking for a lyricist.

I even find poetry writing enjoyable on occasion. If you are at all like me, you will be able to follow in my footsteps to some degree and achieve success. A lot of people will be thrilled to read what you've written.

19. Cycling

Instead of jogging or running, you could go for a ride in the evening on your estate. Go on a weekend hike with the family to learn about new things and see the world in a different light.

Your favorite bike and helmet are already waiting for you in the garage. You can either ride your bike on the road or in the mountains. There is a lot of evidence that shows how beneficial cycling is for your heart and muscles, not to mention how effective it is at toning your legs.

20. Cooking

Spending free time cooking is a productive use of one's time. Preparing meals as a family is a wonderful way to bond while also sharing your passion for trying new foods.

Use the comprehensive video and audio guides offered to successfully attempt something new. Add some flair to your culinary abilities by using your imagination. Start a tradition on the weekend of cooking hearty meals for your family. If you can do it as a pair, you'll have a lot more fun.

Cooking, of course, but also cheesemaking, breadmaking, and home brewing. Take a look at that delicious snack you love so much. Cook it up at home in your own oven. Make baking bread and other baked goods a weekly ritual, and you'll never run out. And you can stop wasting money on unnecessary treats from the supermarket.

21. Creative Art

Think about making coloring, sketching, or painting a regular part of your life if you enjoy these creative pursuits. One or two drawers in every artist's house or studio are reserved for the storage of drawing materials.

If you're having trouble keeping your thoughts in order or finding any motivation, try painting them instead. Having your ideas neatly written down can be very beneficial. It's great that there are so many different tools available for painters to use.

Color mixing is a creative outlet that allows us to let our minds run wild. Make a masterpiece with any type of art supply you like: regular or special crayons, paint, acrylic, watercolors, etc. It's also possible to feel happiness upon viewing a finished painting.

CONCLUSION

Having a hobby or interest that one takes pleasure in can have numerous positive effects on one's life, including a reduction in stress and an increase in a sense of belonging and meaning in one's activities. This is true whether one's hobby of choice is making a sweater for a friend's newborn, skiing on powder, or perfecting a pirouette in ballet class.

A person's interest seems to be renamed as a skill in today's society. It's something you enjoy or have worked hard to master, so you feel confident discussing it. When you commit to something as a "hobby," you automatically set the bar high for yourself in terms of dedication and proficiency. If you aren't, you might as well give up now.

Most people go through phases of disinterest from time to time.

It can be challenging to start a new hobby when we lack motivation and clarity about how to get started. You may have seen lists containing hundreds of potential new hobbies to pursue, but it's easy to feel overwhelmed by so many possibilities. Spending a lot of money on a hobby only to realize a few months in that you hate it was a waste.

Boredom may actually encourage innovation and new ideas, so you shouldn't try to suppress the opportunity just because you're not showing any signs of interest, enthusiasm, or desire.

It's unwise to invest heavily in costly gear before determining whether or not you'll stick with your hobby. Wait to make large purchases until you've settled on a course of action.

If you're having trouble picking between dance and acting as a pastime, try your hand at both! Participate in some dance and acting classes if you're interested. If you're torn between two passions but can't do everything you want to, consider a cross-over like musical theater. Fun and relaxing activities that won't break the bank are always welcome. And when money is tight, they can stand in for the more   expensive   alternatives.

References

"6 Reasons Why Having a Hobby Is Important." *Hobby Value*, hobbyvalue.com/blogs/hobbyvalue-blog/6-reasons-why-having-a-hobby-is-important. Accessed 4 Dec. 2022.

"How to Find Your Hobby." *NewToMoney*, www.newtomoney.com/en/how-to-find-your-hobby. Accessed 4 Dec. 2022.

"20 Ways to Find a Hobby - wikiHow." *wikiHow*, 23 Nov. 2022, www.wikihow.com/Find-a-Hobby.

Ashraf, Layla. "No Hobbies or Interests? Here's What You Should Do." *Medium*, 21 Apr. 2021, shutupandachieve.medium.com/no-hobbies-or-interests-heres-what-you-should-do-dfc8c8d8cc6f.

https://www.careersportal.co.za/general/how-to-find-a-hobby-when-nothing-interestsyou#:~:text=Play%20around%20with%20a%20few,That%20really%20sparks%20your%20interest. Accessed 4 Dec. 2022.

"How to Cope When You've Lost Interest in Everything." *Verywell Mind*, 5 Nov. 2021, www.verywellmind.com/things-to-do-if-you-feel-a-loss-of-interest-5093337.

Ashraf, Layla. "No Hobbies or Interests? Here's What You Should Do." *Medium*, 21 Apr. 2021, shutupandachieve.medium.com/no-hobbies-or-interests-heres-what-you-should-do-dfc8c8d8cc6f.

"I'm Not Good at Anything. What Should I Do? (20+ Great Tips)." *UpJourney*, 17 June 2019, upjourney.com/im-not-good-at-anything-what-should-i-do.

"4 Ways to Find a Hobby You Love." *The Muse*, 1 Sept. 2022, www.themuse.com/advice/how-to-find-a-hobby-you-love.

https://www.inc.com/john-rampton/25-reasons-you-are-not-as-successful-as-you-should-be.html. Accessed 4 Dec. 2022.

"How Hard Is It to Become an Expert at Something?" *Verywell Mind*, 29 Mar. 2022, www.verywellmind.com/expertise-how-hard-is-it-to-become-an-expert-at-something-4173614.

Jones, Ray. "How to Find a Hobby When Nothing Interests You (16 Methods!)." *HobbyFAQS*, 12 Jan. 2022, hobbyfaqs.com/find-hobby.

HobbyKeeda.com. "What Is a Hobby ? Different Types of Hobbies." *Medium*, 8 Nov. 2017, hobbykeeda.medium.com/what-is-a-hobby-different-types-of-hobbies-89083caab43d.

"When You Have No Interests or Hobbies | www.succeedsocially.com." *When You Have No Interests or Hobbies | www.succeedsocially.com*, www.succeedsocially.com/nohobbies. Accessed 4 Dec. 2022.

https://www.careersportal.co.za/general/how-to-find-a-hobby-when-nothing-interests-you#:~:text=Play%20around%20with%20a%20few,That%20really%20sparks%20your%20 interest. Accessed 4 Dec. 2022.

https://www.careersportal.co.za/general/how-to-find-a-hobby-when-nothing-interests-you#:~:text=Play%20around%20with%20a%20few,That%20really%20sparks%20your%20 interest. Accessed 4 Dec. 2022.

Printed in Great Britain
by Amazon

34697717R00056